UYASH

OL. 54

Shonen Sunday E

STORY AND ART BY

MIKO TAKAHAS

CONTENTS

THE STORY THUS FAR

Long ago, in the "Warring States" era of Japan's Muromachi period, dog-like half demon Inuyasha attempted to steal the Shikon Jewel—or "Jewel of Four Souls"—from a village. The village priestess, Kikyo, put a stop to his thievery with an enchanted arrow. Pinned to a tree, Inuyasha fell into a deep sleep, while mortally wounded Kikyo took the jewel with her into her funeral pyre. Years passed...

In the present day, Kagome, a Japanese high school girl, is pulled down into a well and transported into the past. There she discovers trapped Inuyasha—and frees him.

When the Shikon Jewel mysteriously reappears, demons attack. In the ensuing battle, the jewel *shatters*!

Now Inuyasha is bound to Kagome with a powerful spell, and the grudging companions must battle to reclaim the shattered shards of the Shikon Jewel to keep them out of evil hands...

LAST VOLUME Magatsuhi, the evil half of the Shikon Jewel, possesses Kohaku. Inuyasha and Kagome return from modern-day Tokyo to find Miroku collapsed, Sango wounded and Rin unconscious. Kohaku finally repels Magatsuhi from his body and Sesshomaru cuts him down, but a part of Magatsuhi survives. Who is possessed now, Miroku or Rin...?

Now Naraku attempts to absorb Kagome, but Kohaku stabs him with one of her sacred arrows, launching a chain reaction of purification and destruction. In the end, Naraku releases Kagome but steals Kohaku's shard, and Magatsuhi holds Rin hostage...

CHARACTERS

INUYASHA
Half-demon hybrid, son of a human mother and demon father. His necklace is enchanted, allowing Kagome to control him with a word.

KAGOME
Modern-day Japanese schoolgirl who can travel back and forth between the past and present through an enchanted well.

SESSHOMARU
Inuyasha's pure-blood demon half brother. They have the same demon father.

MAGATSUHI
A monstrous demon who dwells inside the Shikon Jewel but can sometimes escape to wreak havoc on everyone.

NARAKU
Enigmatic demon mastermind behind the miseries of nearly everyone in the story. He has the power to create multiple incarnations of himself from his body.

MIROKU
A Buddhist monk cursed with a mystical "Wind Tunnel" imbedded in his hand that both functions as a weapon and is slowly killing him.

SANGO
A demon slayer from the village where the Shikon Jewel originated.

RIN
An orphaned girl devoted to Sesshomaru. He once resurrected her with Tenseiga. She brings out the best in him.

KOHAKU
Kohaku performed Naraku's dirty work for him and is trying to redeem himself.

SCROLL 1
THE JEWEL COMPLETED

RIN HAS...
...BEEN KID-NAPPED?!
IT'S YOUR FAULT, MONK! THAT EVIL AURA THAT SEEPED OUT OF YOUR BODY...
IT SWAL-LOWED THE GIRL UP AND—
EVIL AURA ...?
MAGA-TSUHI...
MAGATSUHI? **HE** TOOK HER?!

JAKEN! HOW COULD YOU LET THIS HAPPEN?! AND RIGHT UNDER YOUR–
SHUT UP!
WHAT TO DO?! SHOULD I RUN?!
WHEN LORD SESSHO-MARU RETURNS... HE'LL KILL ME!
BDMP BDMP BDMP
NOW, WHILE I HAVE THE CHANCE ...
SO. MAGA-TSUHI IS STILL ALIVE...
HOOO...
SESSHO-MARU...
YEEEEEE!

WHAT DO YOU MEAN "STILL ALIVE"...?
DOES THIS HAVE SOMETHING TO DO WITH THE EVIL AURA WITHDRAWING FROM THE MONK'S BODY?
HMPH...
SHOOO...
HE COULD HAVE GIVEN US A HINT AT LEAST!
WHAT A JERK.
DID HE...?
HE DIDN'T EVEN LOOK AT ME...
DOES THAT MEAN... RIN IS IN DANGER?!
MAGATSUHI IS TAKING RIN TO NARAKU.
THE ONLY REASON HE WOULD DO THAT...

...IS TO PREVENT ME
FROM FIGHTING HIM!
FSSH
KOHA-KU!
KOHA-KU!

KOHA-KU!!
IT'S... GONE!
THE SHIKON SHARD THAT WAS MAINTAINING HIS LIFE...
SAN-GO... I... IT'S NOT...
...I CAN'T SAY IT...
KOHA-KU!!

SISTER...
IT'S NOT TOO LATE?!
IS IT...
...ALL RIGHT FOR ME TO...LIVE?
KOHA-KU...
WHY ...?
WHY?!
RRRR...

KAGOME!
WHERE...
...IS NARAKU?!
HOOOO
SSS...
OVER HERE...
HIS BLACK SHIKON JEWEL...
TK

EVEN THOUGH MY ARROW...
KRIII...
...MY SACRED ARROW...
...HAS LOST ITS SPIRIT POWER...
TNG
...IT CAN STILL GUIDE INUYASHA!
SHP
NOW-

MEIDO
ZANGE-
TSUHA!
HSH
SHM

!
HEH HEH HEH... INUYASHA ...

YOU COULDN'T EVEN SAVE LITTLE KOHAKU'S LIFE.
HRROO...
RRR...
KIKYO'S LIGHT HAS DIED OUT.
KOHAKU'S SHARD HAS BEEN THOROUGHLY TAINTED BY ME.
HROO...

SSS...
HE'S RIGHT... I CAN'T MAKE OUT KIKYO'S RAY OF LIGHT ANYMORE!
SROOO....
YOU...

KIKYO AND NOW KOHAKU...
I FAILED THEM!
INU-YASHA ...
I'M SO SORRY...
I'M SORRY, KOHAKU.
WMM
TING...

TINGooo
LIGHT!
COULD IT BE...?
LIGHT... RISING FROM... KOHAKU!
BDMP...

BDMP...
KOHAKU!
KO... HAKU?
SISTER ...?

KIKYO'S LIGHT...
...MUST HAVE ABANDONED THE SHARD TO...STAY IN KOHAKU'S BODY!
KIKYO...
I'LL USE KOHAKU'S SHARD...
...TO EXORCISE NARAKU IN ONE FELL SWOOP.
BUT SHE CHOSE...
...TO SAVE KOHAKU'S LIFE...
...INSTEAD OF DESTROYING NARAKU.

WHICH MEANS THE BATTLE AGAINST NARAKU...
HOOOOO...
...HAS BEEN LEFT TO US!
KCCH...

SCROLL 2
GRADUATION

AT FIRST, IT WAS MERELY THE PITIFUL DREAM OF A CRIPPLED BANDIT...
KIKYO...
TO ESCAPE FROM THE CAVE WITH THE BEAUTIFUL PRIESTESS...
...WAS ALL HE DESIRED.

TO LIVE HIS DREAM, HE ALLOWED DEMONS TO DEVOUR HIS BODY.
AS THEY SWARMED UPON HIM, THEY MERGED INTO ONE...
...AND THUS... *NARAKU WAS BORN.*
HOW LONG IT HAS TAKEN, KIKYO...
THE SHIKON JEWEL, WHICH WAS MEANT TO VANISH ALONG WITH YOUR REMAINS...
...IS NOW FINALLY IN MY GRASP.

SO FILLED WITH MY DARKNESS...
...THAT THERE IS ALMOST NO SPACE LEFT FOR MAGATSUHI TO RETURN...
NARA-KU...
WHAT DO YOU PLAN TO DO WITH THAT JEWEL?
DO WITH IT...?
HEH...
NOTHING.

BUT...
IT WAS THROUGH ***THEIR*** BOND WITH ME...
...THROUGH THEIR RAGE AND HATRED FOR ME...
...THAT I HAVE BEEN TRANS-FORMED. AND THROUGH THEM THAT I HAVE BEEN ABLE TO...
...COMPLETE THIS TAINTED JEWEL.

AND THUS, THE NATURAL END OF THIS STORY MUST BE...
...THAT MY DARKNESS DEVOURS THEM.
AS FOR WHAT LIES BEYOND THAT...
HSH...

INU-YASHA...
DID YOU...
...LET KAGOME GO BACK THROUGH THE WELL AGAIN?
HAD TO.
I PROMISED HER.
SHE SAID SOME-THING ABOUT TODAY BEING SPECIAL ...
NO WAY!!!

I GOT IN?!
I CAN'T BELIEVE IT!
WELL, YOU WERE ON THE WAITING LIST FIRST...
WHO CARES?! IN IS IN!
BUT YOU MISSED SO MUCH SCHOOL!
MAYBE I'M A GENIUS!
HEE HEE
'MORNING!
KAGOME!
YOU ALL GOT IN TOO, RIGHT?
RIGHT?
YOU WERE THE ONLY ONE IN DANGER OF NOT MAKING IT!
CONGRATS GRADUATES
I'M SO HAPPY!
WHEE WHEE

TODAY IS THE DAY...
...AND NOW THE GRADUATES WILL ENTER...
CLAP CLAP CLAP CLAP CLAP CLAP
...I GRADUATE FROM JUNIOR HIGH!
NEXT...
CLAP CLAP CLAP CLAP CLAP CLAP
SNIF
CLAP CLAP CLAP CLAP
CONGRATS
KLIK

HIGU-RASHI!
OH...
HOJO?
I KNOW WE'RE GOING OUR SEPARATE WAYS, BUT...
WE ARE?
HE'S GOING TO AN ALL-BOYS SCHOOL!
D'YOU THINK HE STILL HAS FEELINGS FOR KAGOME?
PSS PSS
PROB-ABLY.
PSS PSS PSS PSS
DOES HE KNOW SHE'S GOT A RUFFIAN FOR A BOYFRIEND?
...CAN WE STILL BE FRIENDS?
OF COURSE!
FRIENDS FOREVER, RIGHT?
POOR THING.

HOOOO...
THE LIGHT HAS DIED.

HOO

DDMM
DDMM DDMM
YOU'RE LEAVING ALREADY, KAGOME?
YUP.
CAN'T YOU AT LEAST STAY FOR DINNER?
WELL, I KINDA FORCED THEM TO LET ME COME BACK HERE, SO...

BUT HEY, GRANDPA...!
DON'T FORGET TO GET ME A GRADUATION PRESENT!
I ALREADY DID.
REALLY?!
A PICKLED DRAGON'S TAIL...
AND THE WHISKERS OF A DOG DEMON.
TA-DAA
ONE'S FOR GRADUATING.
THE OTHER'S FOR GETTING INTO HIGH SCHOOL.
SHOVE
GREAT.
YOU CAN GIVE ME A FANCY PEN SET WHEN I GET BACK.
KAGOME...

GOOD JOB.
CONGRATULATIONS.
MOM ...
THANK YOU...
HSH...

THERE ARE DEMONS ON THE MOVE.
IT'S AS IF...
THEY'RE BEING DRAWN BY SOMETHING...
HOOOOO
AN EVIL AURA IS SPREADING ACROSS THE SKY.
...
LORD INUYASHA... DID NARAKU USE...
...THE JEW-EL?
YEAH. HE DID.

THE TIME TO SETTLE THIS ONCE AND FOR ALL HAS FINALLY COME, EH, NARAKU...?
YOU'VE FEARED KIKYO'S LIGHT FOR SO LONG...AND NOW IT'S BECOME KOHAKU'S LIFE.
KIKYO WON'T BE BATTLING YOU EVER AGAIN.
THAT'S WHY I...
...WHY **WE**... HAVE TO END THIS—NOW.
INU-YASHA!

I'M ALL DONE!
THANK YOU!
GOOD. WE'VE BEEN WAITING FOR YOU. NOW...
HOOOO
IT'S TIME!

SCROLL 3
CLOUD OF EVIL

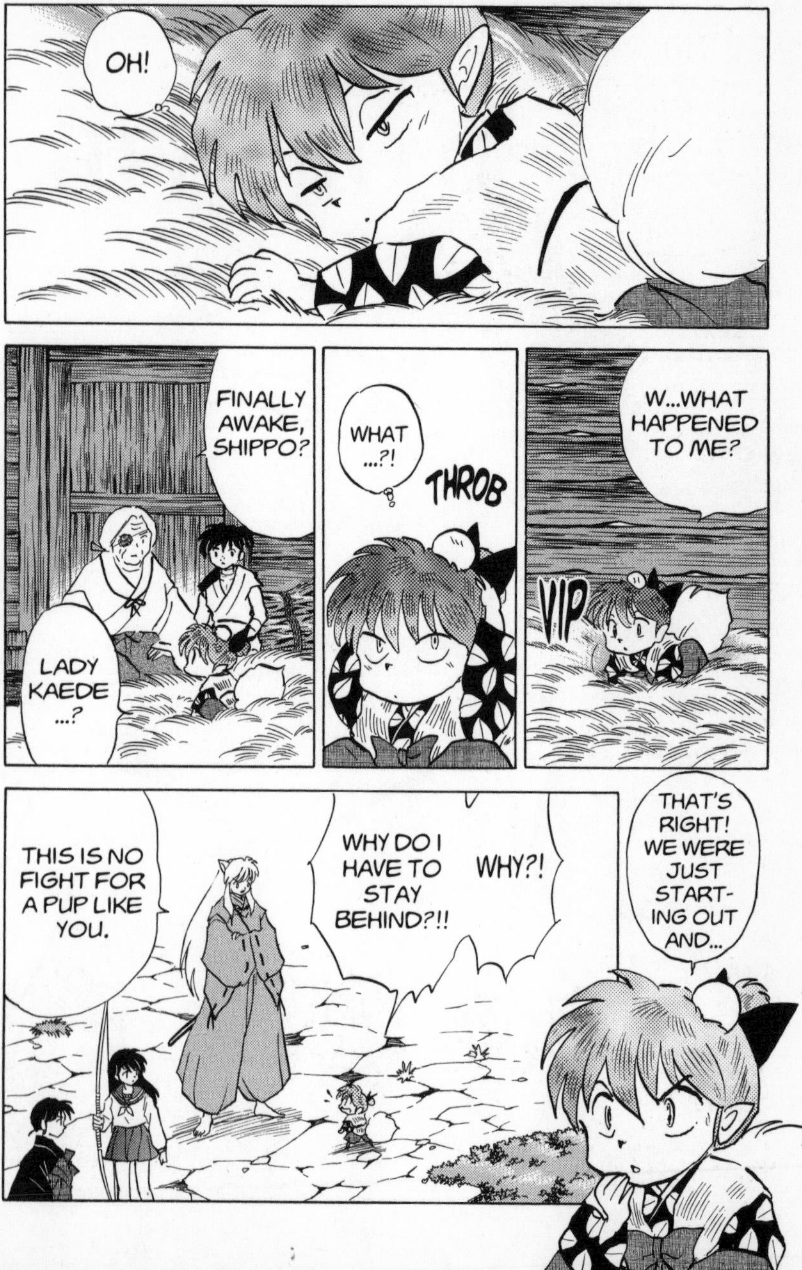
OH!
FINALLY AWAKE, SHIPPO?
LADY KAEDE ...?
WHAT ...?!
THROB
VIP
W...WHAT HAPPENED TO ME?
THIS IS NO FIGHT FOR A PUP LIKE YOU.
WHY DO I HAVE TO STAY BEHIND?!!
WHY?!
THAT'S RIGHT! WE WERE JUST START-ING OUT AND...

THIS BATTLE WILL BE DIFFERENT FROM ANY WE'VE FOUGHT BEFORE, SHIPPO.
NARAKU HAS USED THE SHIKON JEWEL TO TRANSFORM HIMSELF EVEN MORE DRASTICALLY....
I'LL HAVE MY HANDS FULL PROTECTING KAGOME NOW THAT HER POWERS ARE GONE.
I CAN'T KEEP AN EYE ON YOU TOO!
SORRY, SHIPPO.
KOHAKU— YOU TOO.
WE NEED YOU TO STAY WITH LADY KAEDE.
SIS-TER...
DON'T YOU DARE...
...WASTE THE LIFE KIKYO BESTOWED ON YOU!
I WON'T.
BUT...
...WHY?!

HAVEN'T WE FOUGHT SIDE BY SIDE SINCE THE BEGINNING?
AREN'T I ONE OF YOU?
YOU ARE.
YOU ARE ONE OF US, SHIPPO.
THAT'S WHY...
...IF NONE OF US MAKE IT BACK...
...WE'LL NEED YOU TO TAKE CHARGE.
HUH?
TAKE CHARGE?
ME?
YOU'VE GOT THE MAKINGS OF A GREAT DEMON LEADER.

DO YOU UNDER-STAND, SHIPPO?
THEY LEFT WHILE I WAS KNOCKED OUT!!
NO FAIR!
VM
DO YOU UNDER-STAND?!
KONG!
BUT...
SHP
INU-YASHA, YOU IDIOT!!
TNG
YOU'LL NEVER CATCH UP TO THEM NOW.

HOOO...
!

THE EVIL AURA IS SPREADING.
YES...
INU-YASHA...!

SHHH
I DO FEEL KIND OF SORRY FOR SHIPPO THOUGH.
FEH.
THAT WASN'T LIKE YOU, INU-YASHA...
...GIVING VOICE TO SUCH PESSIMISM...
WHAT?!
...IF NONE OF US MAKE IT BACK...
IT WAS THE ONLY WAY TO SHUT HIM UP!
OH, PLEASE!

ASIDE FROM HITTING HIM, YOU MEAN?
HMPH...
I SHOULD'VE JUST CLOCKED HIM IN THE FIRST PLACE!
IT'S TRUE THAT WE'RE GOING TO BE IN REAL DANGER...
WITH MY SPIRIT POWERS SEALED OFF BY MAGATSUHI... AND NO IDEA IF THEY'LL EVER RETURN...
YEAH...
AT THE VERY LEAST, NOT UNTIL SESSHO-MARU WIELDS TENSEIGA...
...AND DESTROYS MAGATSUHI ONCE AND FOR ALL.
HOOO...

NARAKU...

VOOO...

SO...
STILL JUST A BIG SPIDER, I SEE.
HSH
BAKUSAIGA!
SHK

BLIP
BLIP
BLIP
DZZZ
KT
WHAT A REMARKABLE BLADE...
IT CONTINUES TO CONSUME A BODY...
BYAKUYA OF THE DREAMS ...
...EVEN AFTER IT'S BEEN RENDERED A CORPSE.
SO IF NARAKU REABSORBS SUCH A CORPSE, HE'LL BE CONSUMED AS WELL... CORRECT?

IF YOU USE BAKUSAIGA, EVEN THE TRANSFORMED NARAKU...
...WON'T STAND A CHANCE.
SO WHY DON'T YOU GET ON WITH IT? ATTACK HIM!
WOOOO
BDM
BDM

AH. CON-CERNED ABOUT THAT LITTLE GIRL OF YOURS?
YES, WELL, AS YOU SUSPECT ...
...SHE'S THERE.
INSIDE NARAKU.
SPYUU
KKKK
HSH

ZZZZZZZ
VSH
BLP
BLP BLP
VVN
HERE THEY ARE...
THAT SPIDER...
IT'S NARA-KU!

HOLD ON, KAGOME!
VM
!
HOOO
SSS...
ZZZZ!
KRIII...
BLP
BLPBLP

YAAAAW
THE SPIDER IS... OPENING?!

SCROLL 4

INSIDE NARAKU

YAAAAAW

BUT WHY...?
HE'S LEFT HIMSELF WIDE OPEN!

VM
SESSHO-MARU?!
RUSHING IN TO SAVE HER WITHOUT A MOMENT'S HESITATION.
HOW TOUCHING.
BYAKUYA!
HSH
RIN IS... INSIDE?!

LET'S GO, INUYASHA!
VP
YEAH!
SAN-GO?
HSH
WE'RE WITH YOU!
YOU TWO ARE GOING IN AS WELL?
EVEN THOUGH YOU RISK BEING DEVOURED THE MOMENT YOU ENTER?
SSSS...
COME NOW!
I WON'T BE SO EASY TO CATCH WITH YOUR LITTLE WIND TRICK!
ZZIP
RELAX...
YOU'RE NOT WORTH THE EFFORT.
...

THE WIND TUNNEL HAS REACHED ITS LIMIT.
SSS...
I CAN ONLY USE IT ONCE... PERHAPS TWICE MORE...
AND THEN, IT'LL SPLIT OPEN...
...AND I MYSELF WILL BE SWALLOWED UP BY IT—AND VANISH FOREVERMORE.
MY ONLY HOPE IS TO DESTROY NARAKU HERE...
...AND END THE CURSE OF THE WIND TUNNEL.
MONK...
WE'RE GOING TO DEFEAT HIM...
...WITHOUT FAIL!

YES, SANGO.
AND WHEN IT'S ALL OVER AND WE RETURN HOME...
...LET'S BE MARRIED.
HOOOO
...YES.
AND SO THEY ALL DIVE IN...
SILLY THINGS.
TO THINK THEY COULD HAVE JUST SACRIFICED THAT CHILD...
...AND SIMPLY DESTROYED NARAKU FROM THE OUTSIDE.

HOOOO
NARAKU SEEMS...
...A LOT BIGGER ON THE INSIDE THAN THE OUTSIDE...
MM-HM.
!
THAT'S...
GLINT

NARAKU!
SO, INUYASHA... YOU'RE FINALLY...
...RIGHT WHERE I WANT YOU...
!

DMMM
YOU THINK TO DESTROY ME FROM THE INSIDE?
YOU'RE WEL- COME TO TRY.
BUT EVERYTHING AROUND YOU...
...IS... ME.
!
BLP
HIRAI- KOTSU!
VRR

D-DM
SPYUU...
FSH FSH
FSH
SHHHH...
BLP
BLP
MIASMA!
PFF
WHY SO SKITTISH NOW?
SURELY YOU REALIZE...

...THAT FROM THE MOMENT YOU ENTERED ME, YOU'VE BEEN BATHING...
...IN MY MIASMA.
AND YET...NONE OF YOU ARE DEAD.
DMMM
WHY DO YOU SUPPOSE THAT IS...?
BECAUSE THE SHIKON JEWEL DESIRES **YOUR SOULS.**
OUR... SOULS?
THE RAGE THAT FILLS YOUR HEARTS...
...THE HATE AND...
...THE DES-PAIR.

DESPAIR ...?
LIKE HELL!
I'M ABOUT TO SET MYSELF FREE OF YOU— FOREVER!
HEH HEH HEH... TO ACCOMPLISH THAT...
...YOU MUST FIRST DEFEAT THE SHIKON JEWEL.
DO YOU IMAGINE YOU CAN SEVER IT...?
...THE BOND OF THE SHIKON JEWEL, WHICH HAS ENDURED FOR HUNDREDS OF YEARS?

!
SHLP
HOOOO

THIS TOO...IS NARAKU ?!
HIS ENTIRE BODY IS ENCLOSED IN ARMOR!
SSSS
KRIII...

SHP
SIGH...
NOW IT'S AS IF YOU'RE ENTRAPPED IN A JEWEL YOUR-SELVES...

HISH
HYAAA!!
WAK
NGH!

DMM-M
HSH
NOW, INUYASHA... LET US DO BATTLE.
WE HAVE PLENTY OF TIME...
...INSIDE MY BODY.
ACTUALLY... WE HAVE ALL ETERNITY.

SCROLL 5
A TRACE OF THE JEWEL

TK TK SHHHHH
SHMM

HWK
HYOH!!
RRGH ...
TT TT TT TT
SHH
!
SHUK

WMP
ZZZZ
INU-YASHA!
HEH HEH HEH... YOU OUGHT TO KNOW BY NOW...
...THAT TETSUSAIGA IS NO MATCH FOR MY ARMOR.
SHHH

HRR
WHAT ABOUT HIRAIKOTSU?!
THK THK
OZZ...
SSS
DP
HIS HEAD ...!
HER ABILITY TO SLASH AURAS! IS HE...?!

BLIP
BLIP
BLIP
BLUP
BLUP
BLUP
!
HE JUST... SPLIT...

DMMMMM
SHING
DIAMOND SPEARS!!
HSH

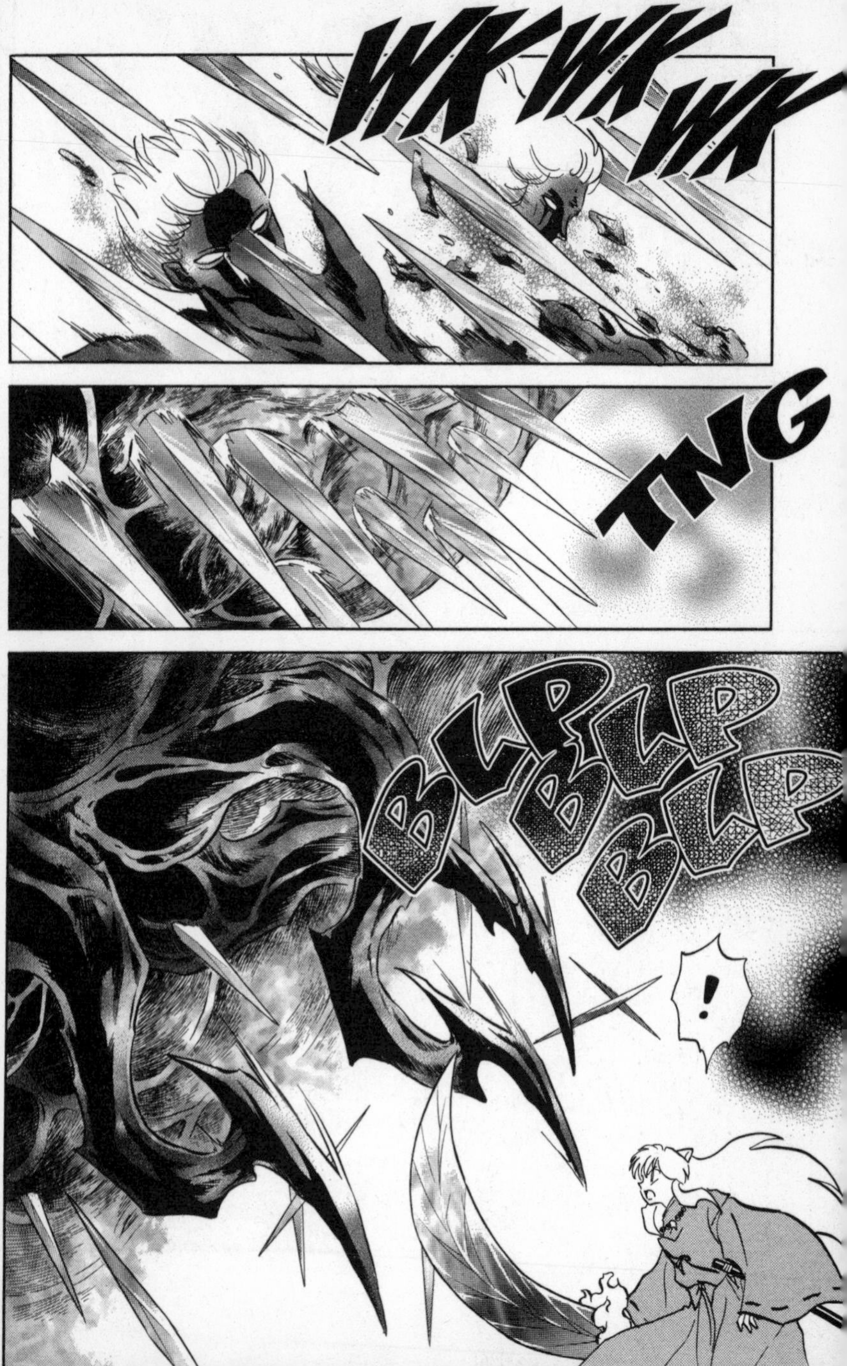
WK WK WK WK
TNG
BLP BLP BLP BLP
!

THIS IS POINTLESS!
MEIDO ZANGE-TSUHA!
TOOM
SENDING ME TO THE UNDER-WORLD, ARE YOU?
GLEEM...
I... I SEE SOME-THING OVER THERE...
!

GLEEM...
THAT'S...
RIN!
SO...THE CHILD HAS AWAKENED.
IT'S JUST ANOTHER ONE OF YOUR ILLUSIONS!
PER-HAPS...

THEN YOU SHOULD STRIKE, SHOULDN'T YOU?
SWEEP ME INTO THE UNDER-WORLD—ILLUSION AND ALL!
RRRR...
NNH...
VSSH
MOVE!
WMMM

HEH HEH HEH... WHAT'S THE MATTER...?
THE CHILD IS SESSHOMARU'S COMPANION.
SHE'S NO CONCERN OF YOURS, INUYASHA.
AND YET...YOU STILL WON'T CUT ME DOWN?
HEH HEH HEH...
WMM
DON'T WORRY. IN A MOMENT YOU'LL BE EAGER TO CUT ME...
...TO SAVE SOMEONE FAR *MORE* IMPORTANT TO YOU.
TO SAVE... *YOURSELF*.
THE JEWEL ...
WE HAVE TO FIND AND DESTROY IT!
THEN NARAKU CAN'T—

THE JEWEL?!
DM
I THOUGHT...
...NARAKU ALREADY ABSORBED THE JEWEL?!
HE DID! AND I THOUGHT IT DISSOLVED INTO HIS BODY!
BUT NOW...
I CAN SENSE IT! DEEP INSIDE HIM!
I THINK THE JEWEL IS STILL INTACT!
WHOA!
WD
WD
!
SHH

VSH
KAGOME!
INU-YASHA!
AGH!
SHOOP
HWP WP
!
IS HE TRYING TO DIVIDE US?!
BLOCKED...

DMMM...
DAMN IT...
KAGOME! WHICH WAY...
...IS THE JEWEL ?!
DMMM
I SENSE IT... STRONGER THAN BEFORE...
THAT WAY...
LET'S GO!
VSH
WE DON'T HAVE TIME TO REACH MIROKU AND SANGO!
BUT WHY...
...IS NARA-KU...?

NARAKU CAN MANIPULATE EVERYTHING INSIDE HIS BODY.
DMMM
SO WHY WOULD HE EVEN LET US GET NEAR THE JEWEL...?
DMMMM
DM M
SHUDDER...

TK
TK
INU-YASHA ...
SSS
YAAAH!!
WHM
WHAT HAP-PENED ...?

HSSSS...
DIDN'T YOU REALIZE...
BLOP
...WHAT WOULD HAPPEN IF YOU APPROACHED THE JEWEL I TAINTED?
INUYASHA IS A FEEBLE HALF DEMON...
THE JEWEL'S POISON HAS SWALLOWED UP HIS HEART.
INU-YASHA ...

SCROLL 6

THE MIASMA ARROW

DMMM
I-INU-YASHA...
SSSH...
SNAP OUT OF IT, INUYASHA!
VZZZ

OH...!
SPYU
SHZ
AAAAH !!
VSH
NGH...
WHAT'S THE MATTER, KAGOME ...?
BECAUSE YOUR SPIRIT POWERS ARE STILL SEALED OFF BY MAGATSUHI!
SKWK SKWK
HEH HEH HEH... YOU CAN'T, CAN YOU?
WHY DON'T YOU USE YOUR PRIESTESS POWERS TO CLEANSE HIS SOUL, HM...?

DOMMM
SKWK SKWK
IF I CAN JUST GET HIM AWAY FROM THE JEWEL...
...MAYBE HE'LL REVERT...
SKWK
SKWK
IT'S NO USE RUNNING ...
!
THE ONLY THOUGHT IN HIS HEAD NOW IS TO KILL YOU.
ZOP...

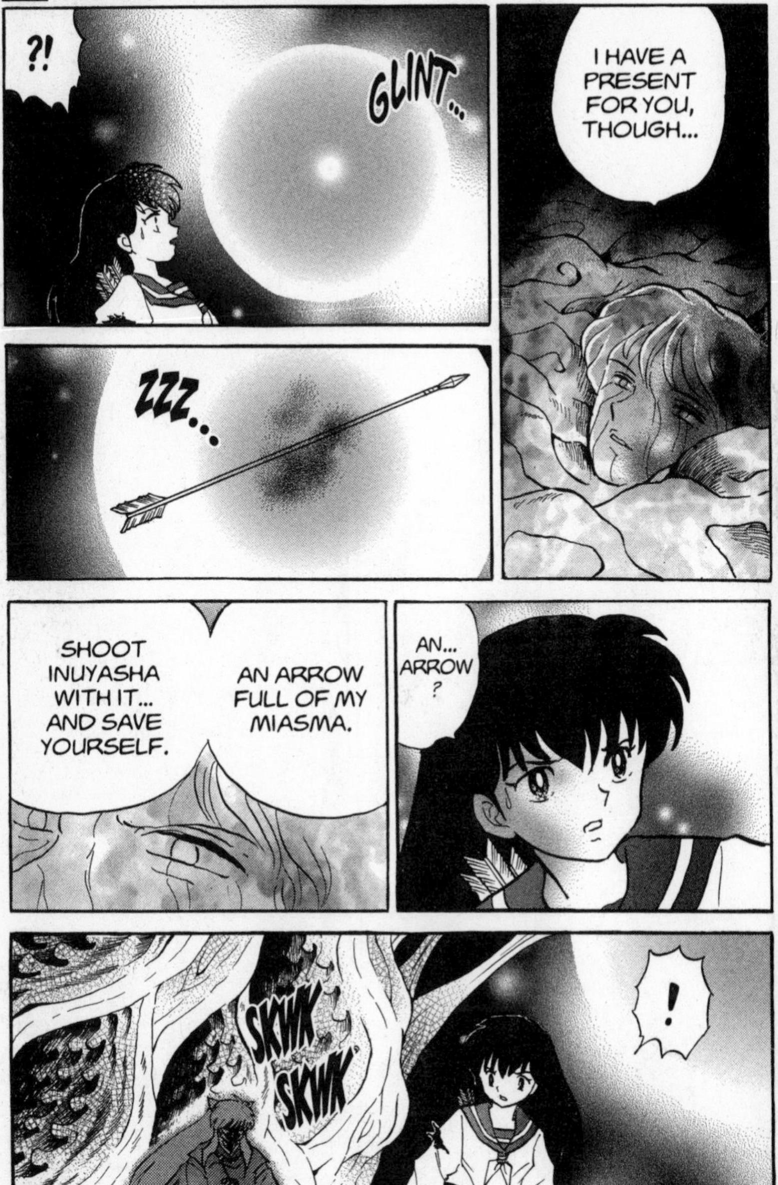
I HAVE A PRESENT FOR YOU, THOUGH...
?!
GLINT...
ZZZ...
AN... ARROW?
AN ARROW FULL OF MY MIASMA.
SHOOT INUYASHA WITH IT... AND SAVE YOURSELF.
!
SKWK SKWK

NHH!
VSH
VSH
!
SKRIK
WRRR...
HOOOO
INU-YASHA ...
RRR...

DMMM
!
WELL ...?
YOU WOULD ALLOW HIM TO KILL YOU?
NARAKU...
...YOU'RE A FOOL.
YOU THINK ***ANYTHING*** WOULD INDUCE ME TO SHOOT INUYASHA?!
OR THAT INUYASHA WOULD EVER—
KILL ***YOU?***
HEH HEH HEH... WE SHALL SEE... VERY SHORTLY!
VSH

WMM
!
INU...
YASHA...
SHH...
RRRR...
HEH
HEH
HEH...
DMMM
WHO IS
THE
FOOL...?

HOOO...
DMMM...
OOO...
WHERE ARE WE... WITHIN NARAKU'S BODY?
LADY KAGO-ME SAID ...
...THE SHIKON JEWEL WAS DEEP INSIDE HIM, BUT...
SSSS...
THE SOUND OF HIS WIND TUNNEL...
IT'S EXPANDED SO MUCH THAT I CAN HEAR IT...

HE HASN'T SAID ANYTHING, BUT...
...THE NEXT TIME HE USES IT... MIGHT BE THE...
LORD MONK ...
SOME-THING WRONG, SANGO?
THIS... MIST...
!
SHOO...

HASSSHH
SSS
WHAT...?!
IT'S...AN ILLU-SION...
I'VE BEEN HERE BEFORE...
MONK MUSHIN'S TEMPLE...
...WHERE I WAS RAISED... AFTER MY FATHER'S DEATH.

NARAKU...
...WHAT ARE YOU PLOTTING NOW?!
THERE HE IS...
THE MONK MUSHIN AND...
...THAT CHILD...

HOOOO...
TP...
THIS IS...
...THAT DAY!
HOOM

RRRRRRKKKK
SHOOOOO
DADDY!
YOU CANNOT GO THERE, MIROKU!
OOO
YOU'LL BE PULLED INTO YOUR FATHER'S WIND TUNNEL AS WELL!
DADDY!

SHOOOOO
RRRKKKKKKKK
OOOO...
NO!

DMMMM...
NO!!
SAN-GO...
BRR RR RR
DO NOT BE FOOLED.
THIS IS ALL A TRICK.
BUT IT...
...IT WAS SO...

NARAKU...
WHY SHOW ME THIS VISION NOW?
OR...
WERE YOU SHOWING IT TO SANGO?!
!
SHK SHK SHK SHK

HOOO...
DMMM
DMMM

SCROLL 7

NARAKU'S DARKNESS

INU-
YASHA!
WHY DID
YOU
BETRAY
ME?!
WD
KIKYO...
I DIDN'T
KNOW.
WE BOTH FELL INTO
NARAKU'S TRAP. HE
SET US UP TO HATE
EACH OTHER.
AND
THEN...YOU
CHASED
AFTER ME...
FOLLOWED
ME INTO
DEATH...

KIKYO, I SWEAR TO PROTECT YOU THIS TIME.
I WILL NEVER LET NARAKU HURT YOU AGAIN!
SKWIK
HOO...
AND THEN...
SSSH...
...I FAILED HER AGAIN.

INU-
YASHA...
TP...
INUYASHA.
KAGO-
ME...?
I WILL
ALWAYS BE
AT YOUR
SIDE.
KAGOME...
I SWEAR...
I'LL GIVE MY LIFE TO
PROTECT YOU.
THIS TIME...
I WON'T...

INU-YASHA ...
SHHH...
DMMMM

THAT SCENT...
HST
BLOOD ...
KAGO-ME'S BLOOD ...?!
DON'T YOU REMEM-BER...?
ZWP
ZWP
I SUPPOSE NOT...
...SINCE YOU'VE HARDLY BEEN YOURSELF OF LATE.

NARAKU...
WHAT DID YOU DO TO KAGOME ?!
HEH HEH HEH... HOW POIGNANT.
DON'T YOU REMEMBER RIPPING APART THE WOMAN YOU LOVE?
I... WHAT...?!
YOU'VE DONE IT AGAIN, INUYASHA.
NOT ONLY DID YOU FAIL TO PROTECT YOUR WOMAN...

...BUT KAGOME, LIKE KIKYO...
...BECAME A BLOOD SACRIFICE TO YOUR WEAK-NESS.
SHUT UP!
WOK
I KILLED KAGOME ...?!
IT'S A LIE!
WOK
DMM
DMMM...
KAGO-ME...

INU-YASHA...
ALLOW ME TO LIBERATE YOU FROM YOUR GREATEST WEAKNESS.
DMMM
FORGET IT ALL... FORGET KAGOME...
...AND YOUR HUMAN HEART.
DMMM
KNOW THE PURE JOY OF KILLING.
THAT... IS WHAT THE JEWEL DESIRES FOR YOU.

HOOO...
NNH...
ZSH

OWW...
SESSHO-MARU...?
HWP
VSH
YOU'VE BEEN... PROTECTING ME...?
THAT WOUND ...

...IT'S FROM INU-YASHA'S CLAWS, ISN'T IT?
SO THE HALF DE-MON...
...HAS BEEN SWAL-LOWED UP BY NARAKU'S DARK-NESS.
N-NO...
...INU-YASHA IS...
SKWK
OH...!
HEY, WAIT UP!
SKWK SKWK
IN THAT MOMENT, INU-YASHA...

HE HELPED ME ESCAPE...
...BEFORE HE COMPLETELY LOST CONTROL.
...PUSHED ME AWAY.
ISN'T THAT RIGHT... INUYASHA?
HOOO.....

ZHOOO
RGH!
FCH
BLUP
BLP BLP

THE MORE OF THEM WE DESTROY, THE MORE THEY MULTIPLY!
THERE'S NO END OF THEM!
ZZZZ
VSH
KIRARA!
OUR ONLY CHOICE IS TO FLEE!
BECAUSE IF MIROKU FEELS COMPELLED TO USE HIS WIND TUNNEL AGAIN...
...HE'LL END UP LIKE HIS FATHER...

SHUUU
!
HWP
WOK
OHH!
BAM

SAN-GO!
WOM
TAKA TAKA
UNH...
HZZZ
!

!
HIRAI-KOTSU...
VSH
RGH...
THERE'S NO TIME!
JAKA
NO!
DON'T, LORD MONK!

SCROLL 8

THE WIND TUNNEL'S LIMIT

IT WILL KILL YOU!
KLATTER

BLP
BLP
BLP
WIND TUNNEL!
OOO

OOOOOOOOO
SHLP
LP LP

UGH!
BRRRRRRRR
SPLSH
SPLSH
HH!
NO!
LORD MONK!!

JAKA
UNH!
LORD MONK!
STAY BACK, SANGO!
!
NNN

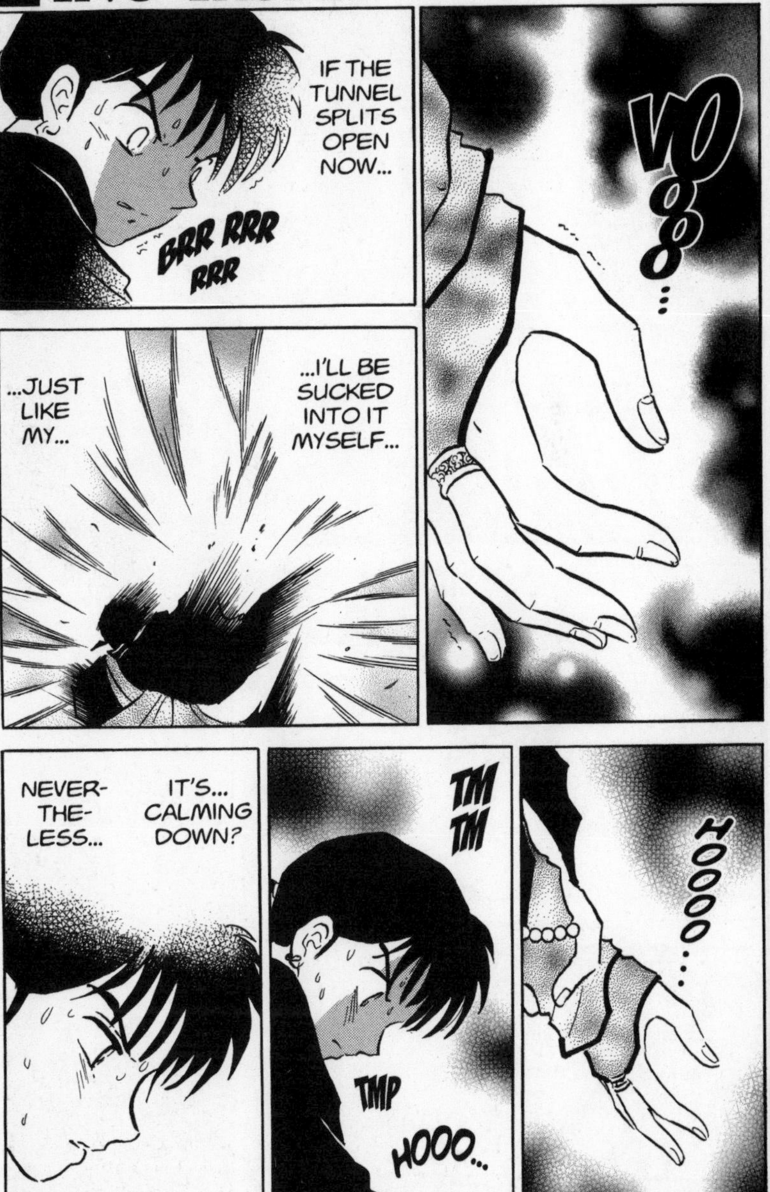
VOOO...
IF THE TUNNEL SPLITS OPEN NOW...
BRR RRR RRR
...I'LL BE SUCKED INTO IT MYSELF...
...JUST LIKE MY...
HOOOOO...
TM TM
TMP
HOOO...
IT'S... CALMING DOWN?
NEVER-THE-LESS...

LORD MONK ...
SKWK
SANGO... HERE WE MUST PART WAYS.
WHAT ...?!
...THE TIME...
...HAS COME!!

KIRA-RA!
KIRA-RA!
MONK, NO!
WAIT!
VZ
VSH
MEW!
SSH

LORD MONK ...!
MIROKU!
SKWK
FORGIVE ME, SANGO...
THE WIND TUNNEL IS ABOUT TO...SPLIT OPEN.
HOOOOO
AND WHEN THAT HAPPENS, NOT JUST I...
...BUT YOU, TOO, WOULD FALL PREY TO IT.
AND THAT...
...WOULD BE MORE PAINFUL TO ME THAN DEATH ITSELF.

HOOOOO...
LADY KAEDE, IS THAT...?
HSH...
YES. IT'S NARAKU... TRANSFORMED.
IT'S AS IF...
...HE HAS *BECOME* THE SHIKON JEWEL!

HOOOO...
...IF NONE OF US MAKE IT BACK...
...WE'LL NEED **YOU** TO TAKE CHARGE.
HOW LONG AM I SUPPOSED TO WAIT...?
I KNEW I SHOULD'VE GONE WITH THEM...
HEH.
EASY FOR YOU TO SAY...
...WHEN YOU'RE JUST SITTING AROUND HERE.

OH YEAH? SO WHAT ARE **YOU** DOING HERE, JAKEN?
YOU AREN'T AFRAID TO JOIN THE BATTLE, ARE YOU...?
OF COURSE NOT!
WHILE I WAS SITTING DEEP IN THOUGHT, CONSIDERING HOW BEST I MIGHT CONTRIBUTE TO THE STRUGGLE, THEY ALL SLIPPED AWAY! BY THE TIME I REALIZED WHAT HAD HAPPENED, IT WAS ALREADY TOO—
OH SAVE IT!!
HOOO
...
SHIPPO ...
...YOU CAN FLOAT, CAN'T YOU?
WHY DON'T YOU TAKE ME UP TO THAT BLACK BALL IN THE SKY.
I REALLY SHOULD BE AT MY LORD'S SIDE...

HEY! DON'T YOU DARE LEAVE WITHOUT ME!
YAH!
JAB
WHADDYA THINK YOU'RE DOING?!
BONG
UM...
HM?
TK

HOOO...
DMMM
SESSHO-MARU...
YOU'VE GOT A SHARP NOSE...
WHY...
...CAN'T YOU FIND RIN?
NARAKU'S BODY...
...IS IMPOS-SIBLY VAST...
TING...

OH...!
GLEEM...
RIN...
A MERE ILLU-SION.
THERE'S NO SCENT.
THIS IS ABSURD...
DOES HE THINK TO MOCK ME...?
HOOOO...
VWOO...

UNH...
W-WHAT... JUST HAPPENED?
WHERE ...?
MAGA-TSUHI ...
BM
VWOO
YAAA!
SKWK SKWK
OOO...
LORD SESSHO-MARU!
LORD SESSHO-MARU, HELP!!
SKWK
SKWK
SKWK
OH!
LORD INU-YASHA!
SKWK SKWK

DMMM
HSSS...
LORD INUYASHA ...?

SCROLL 9

THE LAST BIT OF REASON

SHE'S CLOSE.
WHAT ...?
Oooo
YOU'VE SCENTED RIN...?
WE MUST HURRY.

BM
YAAA!!
HEY!
IS RIN IN DANGER?!
INUYASHA IS ALSO NEARBY.
BUT STILL IN FULL DEMON FORM.
IF INUYASHA HURTS RIN...
SESSHO-MARU WILL NEVER...

HOOOO...
LORD INU-YASHA ...?
SKWK
KRK
YOU ARE...
...LORD INU-YASHA, AREN'T YOU?
VM
HSH

WWOO
EEEE!
SKWK
VZZ
DON'T... MOVE...
HUH ...?!
SWR

WOK
LORD INUYASHA...
SKWK
HEH HEH HEH...
STILL A SCRAP OF HUMAN HEART IN YOU, EH?
WELL...

...NO MATTER.
NRRB
YOU CAN'T EVEN SCRATCH ME.
ZWOOO
G'G'G'G'G'
!

HOOOO...
HE WENT INSIDE LORD INUYASHA!
JUST LIKE WITH KOHAKU ...
HE'S GOING TO TAKE CONTROL OF HIM!
VM
!
LORD SESSHO-
!
ZWP
VOOO

RIN...
SHP
SKWK
9
DMM

HOOOOOO
SSS
INU-YASHA!
HE'S POSSESSED... BY MAGATSUHI...?
SORRY, MAGATSUHI...
YOU PICKED THE WRONG ONE TO POSSESS.
SHINK
TEN-SEIGA!

VM
I'LL CUT YOU DOWN—AND INUYASHA TOO!
DMMMM
THE MEIDO ZANGE-TSUHA!
INUYASHA, STOP!

VSH
HOOO
LORD JAKEN ...
YOU WERE PLANNING TO RIDE SHIPPO UP TO NARAKU?
YOU'VE GOT TRANSPOR-TATION!
SHUSH!
WHY SHOULD I GO IN ALL BY MYSELF?!
YOU WERE AFRAID TO BE ALONE?
SHIPPO IS JUST A CHILD AND HE—
WHO ARE YOU TO CALL ME A CHILD?!
AND WHAT ABOUT YOU...?!
DIDN'T SANGO TELL YOU NOT TO GO?
YES, BUT...
...IT'S TAKING THEM TOO LONG.

OOOO
TH-THAT'S NARAKU...?
I DIDN'T THINK HE'D BE SO...BIG.
BLUP
!

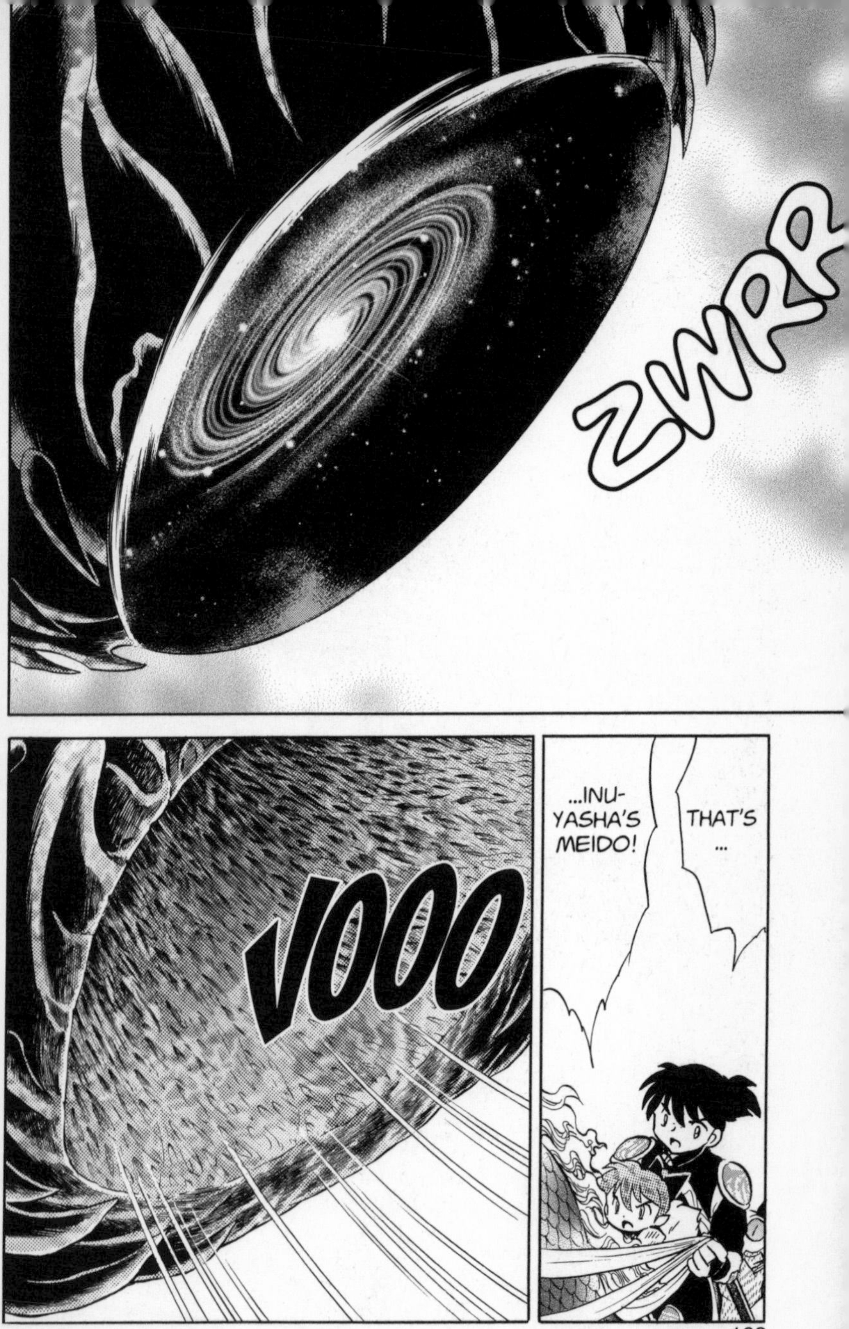
ZWRR
THAT'S ...
...INU-YASHA'S MEIDO!
VOOO

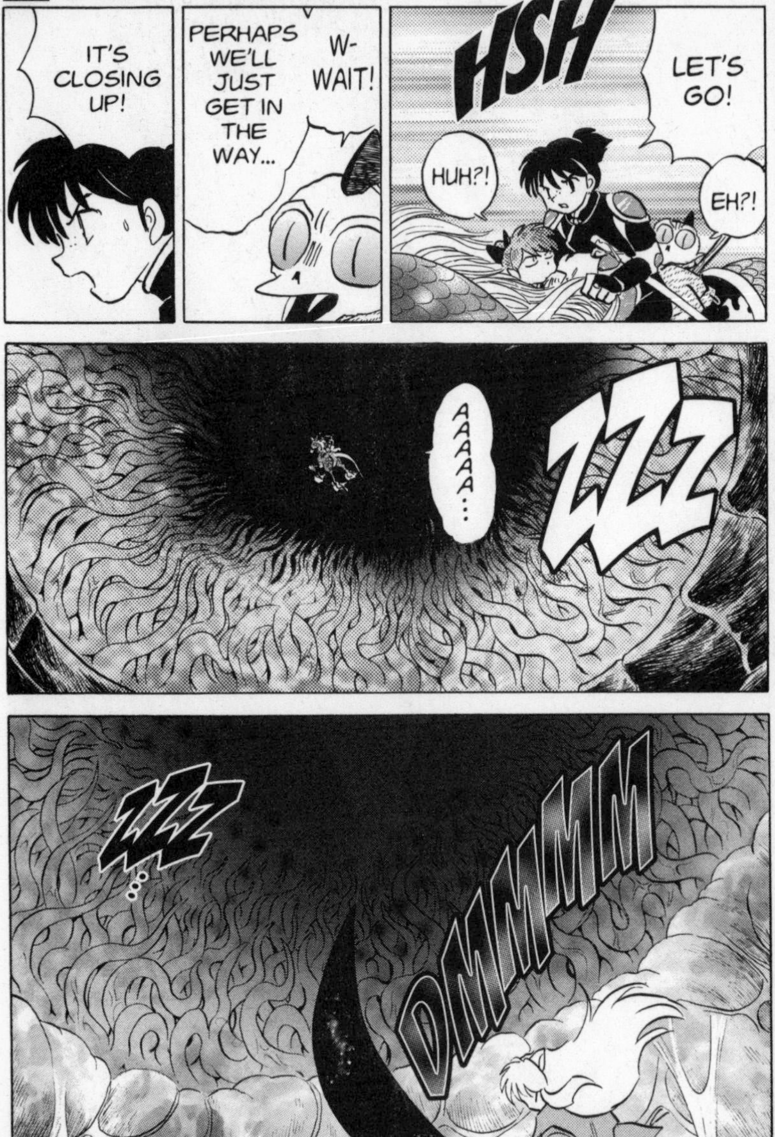
LET'S GO!
HSH
HUH?!
EH?!
W- WAIT!
PERHAPS WE'LL JUST GET IN THE WAY...
IT'S CLOSING UP!
ZZZ
AAAAA...
ZZZ
DMMMM

HOOO
HE MISSED ...
...INTEN-TIONALLY ?!
INU-YASHA ...
OMMM
TETSU-SAIGA...?

THE BLADE IS...
...HELPING INUYASHA HANG ON TO HIS LAST BIT OF REASON!
FP
WD
INU-YASHA !!
TETSU-SAIGA...

BAM
FZZ
DMMM
HE RAN OFF...!
GRAB TETSU-SAIGA!
WE'RE GOING AFTER INUYASHA AND MAGATSUHI!
LET'S GO!

SCROLL 10

THE SCENT OF KAGOME'S BLOOD

ZSH
INSIDE THIS MASS OF FLESH...
...I CATCH THEIR SCENT!
ZASH
MAGATSUHI AND INUYASHA ARE STILL NEARBY!
SESSHOMARU...
...YOU CAN DO IT, RIGHT?!
YOU CAN DEFEAT MAGATSUHI WITHOUT HURTING INUYASHA?

WHEN WE CAME IN HERE, NARAKU TOLD US...
"THE SHIKON JEWEL DESIRES YOUR SOULS...
"THE RAGE THAT FILLS YOUR HEARTS...
"...THE HATE AND...
"...THE DESPAIR..."
ZSH
"THE JEWEL WANTS THE DARKEST PARTS OF YOUR HEARTS."
WHICH IS WHY...
...IF YOU FIGHT YOUR BROTHER, YOU'LL PLAY RIGHT INTO NARAKU'S HANDS!
ZWOP
I BROKE THROUGH ...?!

HNNM
ZSH

STAY BACK!
YOU'LL GET IN MY WAY!
VSH
HWAK
WOK

BMM
SSSS
TM
SHAK

HWP
HWP
PWIK
OH...!
HMPH ...
WITH THE BODY AND HEART OF A FULL DEMON...
...YOU'RE TOUGHER THAN USUAL.

I WOULD BE PLAYING RIGHT INTO NARAKU'S HANDS, EH?
BUT THEN...
...IF I HOLD BACK, I'LL ONLY PROLONG THE INEVITABLE.
I SHOULD JUST FINISH THIS QUICKLY!
TM
HSH
TM
SHH
INU-YASHA!!

GRP
HE GRABBED TENSEI-GA'S BLADE!
TENSEIGA IS USELESS AGAINST CREATURES OF THIS REALM...
INCLUDING INUYASHA...AS LONG AS I OCCUPY HIS BODY.
NNN...

GG
HE'LL JUST **SNAP** THAT BLADE OF YOURS.
WM
VSH
WAM

INU-YASHA...
I'VE GOT TO GET TETSU-SAIGA TO HIM!
SOME-HOW... I'VE GOT TO...
SKFF
NNN...
!
ZHP

YAAA!
ZHOOO
YOU FOOL!
GRP
NGH!
JAB
PLEASE, TETSUSAIGA...
...HOLD ME UP!

SHKK
KKK
INU-YASHA!
DON'T GIVE IN!
I'M COMING!
SSSH...
IT'S TOO LATE.
I HAVE ALREADY TAKEN COMPLETE CONTROL...

...OF INUYASHA'S HEART.
EVEN IF HE WERE TO GRASP TETSUSAIGA AGAIN, NOTHING WOULD CHANGE.
INUYASHA! YOU HAVE TO FIGHT HIM!
INU-YASHA!!
BLOOD...

THE SCENT...
...OF KAGOME'S BLOOD...
I CUT HER.
SHE IS NO MORE.
I SWORE I'D GIVE MY LIFE TO PROTECT HER.
YOU'VE DONE IT AGAIN, INUYASHA.
NOT ONLY DID YOU FAIL TO PROTECT YOUR WOMAN...
...BUT KAGOME, LIKE KIKYO...
...BECAME A BLOOD SACRIFICE TO YOUR WEAKNESS.

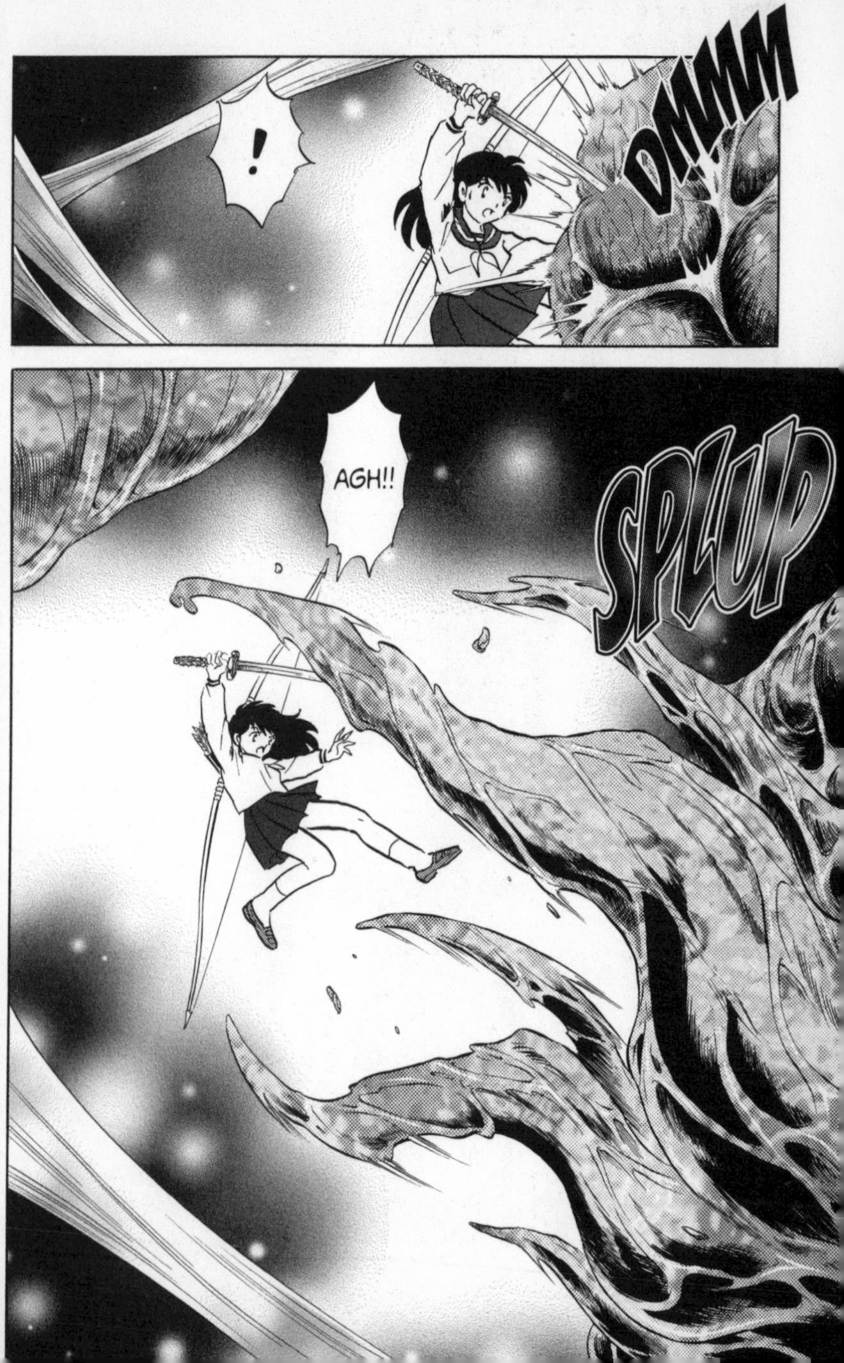
DMMM
!
SPLUP
AGH!!

FEH!
HST
!
VVM
KAGOME!

TO BE CONTINUED...

INUYASHA

INUYASHA
VOL. 54
Shonen Sunday Edition

Story and Art by
RUMIKO TAKAHASHI

Original Japanese edition "INUYASHA"
published by SHOGAKUKAN Inc.

English Adaptation by Gerard Jones
Translation/Mari Morimoto
Touch-up Art & Lettering/Bill Schuch
Cover & Interior Graphic Design/Yuki Ameda
Editor/Annette Roman

Printed in the U.S.A.

Published by VIZ Media, LLC
P.O. Box 77010
San Francisco, CA 94107

10 9 8 7 6 5 4 3 2 1
First printing, November 2010

RATED T+ FOR OLDER TEEN
PARENTAL ADVISORY
INUYASHA is rated T+ for Older Teen and is recommended for ages 16 and up. This volume contains violence.
ratings.viz.com

www.viz.com
WWW.SHONENSUNDAY.COM

InuYasha
The popular anime series now on DVD—each season available in a collectible box set
InuYasha Season 1
InuYasha
InuYasha Third Season Box Set

りんね
RIN-NE
Story and Art by Rumiko Takahashi
he latest series from the creator of
uyasha and Ranma ½
Japan-North America
imultaneous Manga Release!
SHONEN SUNDAY
りんね
RIN-NE
Story and Art by
RUMIKO TAKAHASHI
1
ead a FREE manga
review and order the
raphic novel at
heRumicWorld.com
so available at your local
okstore and comic store
OL. 1 AVAILABLE NOW
BN-13: 978-1-4215-3485-5
.99 US | $12.99 CAN
OUKAI NO RINNE © 2009 Rumiko TAKAHASHI/Shogakukan
WITHDRAWN
viz media
ww.viz.com
RATED T+ FOR OLDER TEEN
ratings.viz.com
MANGA STARTS ON SUNDAY
SHONENSUNDAY.COM
SHONEN SUNDAY